The Real Estate Cloud

By: Matthew Curcio

The Real Estate Cloud

In the rapidly evolving world of real estate, where technology and human interactions intertwine, "The Real Estate Cloud" emerges as a transformative concept that redefines how realtors collaborate with the social media community. This innovative approach envisions a seamless connection between real estate professionals and the ever-present online sphere, granting them unprecedented access to a wider audience, enhanced engagement, and a more personalized client experience.

At its core, "The Real Estate Cloud" represents a dynamic synergy between realtors and social media platforms, harnessing the power of the digital realm to amplify the reach and impact of their services. Just as clouds traverse the sky, the concept of the cloud follows both realtors and potential clients, ensuring that information, listings, and expertise are always accessible, regardless of location or time.

In this collaborative ecosystem, realtors transcend traditional boundaries by integrating themselves into the daily lives of the social media community. They become active participants, sharing insightful content, market updates, and property listings that resonate with users' interests. This not only establishes them as reliable sources of real estate knowledge but also cultivates a sense of trust and familiarity.

"The Real Estate Cloud" takes advantage of the interconnected nature of social media, enabling realtors to engage in meaningful conversations with prospective clients. These interactions transcend the transactional, focusing on building relationships, understanding preferences, and addressing concerns. By listening to the pulse of the community, realtors can tailor their services to meet the evolving needs of their clientele.

Moreover, this collaborative approach fosters a two-way flow of information. Social media users also contribute their insights, sharing local knowledge, experiences, and preferences that provide invaluable context to the real estate process. This interactive exchange creates a vibrant feedback loop, enriching the understanding of both realtors and clients.

As the cloud follows individuals wherever they go, "The Real Estate Cloud" ensures that the real estate journey is continuous and accessible. Whether through immersive virtual property tours, live Q&A sessions, or informative videos, realtors extend their services beyond physical boundaries, accommodating diverse schedules and preferences.

In conclusion, "The Real Estate Cloud" signifies a paradigm shift in the way realtors collaborate with the social media community. It encapsulates the idea of a persistent, interconnected presence that transcends geographical limitations. By embracing this concept, real estate professionals leverage the power of technology and human connection to create a landscape where collaboration, communication, and meaningful engagement thrive, ultimately reshaping the future of the industry.

The Real Estate Cloud [How I got involved in real estate consulting]

After graduating college, I had no idea what I was going to do. I asked friends, family and even strangers for advice (That's how bad it got at one point). I knew I loved to talk, but finding a job in front of a camera was hard and I realized that using my Broadcasting Degree was an unrealistic plan. I worked odd jobs and took exams for jobs at random, looking for anything. It wasn't until a friend told me that I should try phone sales. He told me "You would be great on the phones, in fact you are already great on the phones, you might as well get paid for it." So, I did what most people my age (23) did back in 2017, I applied to work at a few startups in Manhattan. I had first round interviews that eventually led to onsite sit downs, and eventually, I landed a job at a very seed round startup in Midtown East (NYC). I was nervous, but I had nothing to lose. It was here, where I meant my mentor. He helped me, looked after me, trained me, and gave me a 2-week schedule which also had Maslow's Hierarchy of Needs as a whole day topic. I still remember his saying to me:

"You can't understand yourself as a sales rep, if you fail to understand why it is that people do what they do. Are they happy? Are they sad? Are they fulfilled? If yes, great, if not, well, it's your job to understand why they aren't and what you can do to change their life. Got it?"

"Got it!" I told him.

"So, look, we are going to sell our platform and our services to Dentists, Medical Doctors, Chiropractors, and anyone else in the medical field that needs help with their online video presence."

"Got it," I said. "Dentists, Medical Doctors and wait, who else?"

"Chiropractors, but we are open to almost anyone in the medical field."

We tried this for about three weeks. Business was good but it wasn't great. My boss sat me down in a separate room. I thought I was fired, but, we were changing the plan.

"Look, forget about the medical field for now."

"No more Doctors?" I asked.

"For now, let's switch gears, okay? Let's focus on Insurance brokers, Sports Agents and Licensed Realtors."

"Like Real Estate Agents?" I asked.

"Yes, Real Estate Agents, 75 % of our strategy for the next 6 months is going to be realtors and we may sprinkle in some interior designers. Got it?"

"Got it," I said.

A few weeks went by. Business was booming!!!!

"Hey, Matt just curious how are you getting so many realtors on the phone?"

"I'm using Instagram."

"Instagram, huh?" My boss asked. "Well, whatever you're doing, keep doing it, it's working."

And that was how my passion for working with agents was born.

The Real Estate Cloud

In 2021 there were over 2 million licensed real estate agents in the United States. Real Estate is a popular field but for years people have neglected social media often referring to Twitter (Now X), Instagram, LinkedIn, and Tik Tok as a trend that would surely slow down. Wrong.

Social media platforms provide a valuable opportunity for real estate agents to connect with potential clients, showcase properties, and establish their brand. Here are some ways real estate agents use social media:

1. **Property Listings:** Agents often post photos, videos, and descriptions of properties they are representing. This allows them to reach a larger audience and provide potential buyers with a virtual tour of the property.

2. **Engagement:** social media allows agents to engage with their audience through comments, likes, and shares. This interaction helps build relationships and can lead to inquiries about properties or real estate services.

3. **Brand Building:** Agents can use social media to establish their brand identity and showcase their expertise in the real estate market. Sharing informative content about the local market, buying/selling tips, and industry trends can help position them as knowledgeable professionals.

4. **Networking:** Real estate agents can connect with other professionals in the industry, such as mortgage brokers, home inspectors, and

contractors, through platforms like LinkedIn. This networking can lead to valuable referrals and partnerships.

5. **Live Tours and Q&A Sessions:** Agents can use live video streaming to host virtual property tours, answer questions from potential clients, and provide insights into the buying or selling process.

6. **Community Involvement:** Sharing information about local events, neighborhood highlights, and community initiatives can help agents become more integrated within the areas they serve.

7. **Client Testimonials:** Agents can share testimonials and success stories from satisfied clients, which can build trust and credibility among potential clients.

8. **Advertisements:** Social media platforms offer targeted advertising options that allow agents to reach specific demographics and audiences interested in real estate.

9. **Market Updates:** Agents can provide real-time updates about the local housing market, such as new listings, price changes, and market trends.

10. **Educational Content:** Agents can create and share educational content about the real estate process, helping potential buyers and sellers better understand the intricacies of transactions.

It's important for real estate agents to choose the right social media platforms based on their target audience and goals. Platforms like Facebook, Instagram, LinkedIn, and Twitter are commonly used by real estate professionals to connect with clients and showcase their listings.

The Power of 1 New Follower – Be open, be flexible, most importantly be kind…

Here are some of the benefits of one new follower.

1. **Increased Reach:** Each new follower represents an additional person who will see your posts, content, and updates. This extends your online reach and increases the potential for your content to be shared and seen by a wider audience.

2. **Networking and Engagement:** New followers can engage with your content by liking, commenting, and sharing. These interactions not only boost your engagement metrics but also create opportunities for meaningful conversations and connections.

3. **Building a community:** Followers are often individuals who have a genuine interest in your content and expertise. Over time, these followers can become part of your online community, interacting with you and each other, which can foster a sense of loyalty and connection.

4. **Brand Awareness:** Every follower you gain exposes your brand to a larger audience. This is especially important for real estate agents who want to establish themselves as local experts and be top-of-mind when potential clients are ready to buy or sell property.

5. **Social Proof:** A growing follower count can serve as social proof, indicating to others that your content is worth following. People often consider

the number of followers when deciding whether to engage with an account.

6. **Opportunities for Influence:** As your follower count grows, you may gain more influence and credibility within your industry. This could lead to opportunities for partnerships, collaborations, speaking engagements, or media features.

7. **Lead Generation:** Some of your followers could turn into potential clients or referral sources. Sharing valuable content can position you as a trustworthy expert, increasing the likelihood that followers will consider your services.

8. **Feedback and Insights:** Interactions with new followers can provide valuable feedback and insights. They might ask questions, share their preferences, or provide suggestions, which can help you tailor your content and services to better meet their needs.

9. **Algorithmic Benefits:** On platforms like Instagram and Facebook, engagement with your content (likes, comments, shares) often signals to the platform's algorithms that your content is valuable. This can result in your posts being shown to a wider audience, including people who don't yet follow you.

While the power of a single new follower is not monumental on its own, the cumulative effect of gaining multiple followers can significantly impact your online presence and business growth over time. It's important to focus on creating valuable, engaging, and authentic content to attract and retain followers who genuinely resonate with your brand and expertise.

Do These Cities Speak to You?

In the United States, there are several cities that are known for their vibrant and competitive real estate markets. These cities often attract a mix of buyers, investors, and sellers due to factors such as economic growth, job opportunities, lifestyle amenities, and cultural attractions. Here are some of the most popular real estate cities in America:

1. **New York City, New York:** New York City is renowned for its diverse neighborhoods, iconic skyline, and a wide range of real estate options, from luxury condos in Manhattan to historic brownstones in Brooklyn.
2. **Los Angeles, California:** With its entertainment industry, desirable climate, and diverse neighborhoods, Los Angeles offers a range of properties, including luxurious homes in areas like Beverly Hills and beachfront properties in Malibu.
3. **San Francisco, California:** Known for its tech industry and limited housing supply, San Francisco's real estate market is competitive, especially in neighborhoods like Silicon Valley and Pacific Heights.
4. **Miami, Florida:** Miami's tropical climate, beachfront properties, and international appeal attract buyers and investors from around the world, making it a hub for luxury real estate.
5. **Chicago, Illinois:** Chicago's diverse neighborhoods, iconic architecture, and vibrant cultural scene contribute to a dynamic real estate market with

options ranging from historic homes to modern condos.

6. **Boston, Massachusetts:** With its numerous universities, historic sites, and strong job market, Boston's real estate market is competitive, especially in neighborhoods close to downtown and universities.

7. **Seattle, Washington:** The presence of tech giants like Amazon and Microsoft has contributed to Seattle's growth, making it a desirable real estate market for both residential and commercial properties.

8. **Austin, Texas:** Austin's tech industry, live music scene, and lower cost of living compared to other tech hubs have led to a thriving real estate market with increasing demand.

9. **Denver, Colorado:** Denver's strong job market, outdoor recreation opportunities, and quality of life have contributed to a growing real estate market, particularly in desirable neighborhoods.

10. **Nashville, Tennessee:** Nashville's music industry, cultural attractions, and affordability have led to a surge in population growth and a competitive real estate market.

11. **Atlanta, Georgia:** As a major business hub in the Southeast, Atlanta offers a mix of urban and suburban real estate options, catering to a diverse range of buyers.

12. **Washington, D.C.:** The nation's capital has a unique real estate market due to its political and government-related activities, attracting a mix of professionals and diplomats.

It's important to note that real estate market conditions can change over time due to economic factors, population shifts, and other influences. Each city's real estate market has its own nuances and trends, so consulting with local real estate professionals can provide the most accurate and up-to-date information about specific markets.

The Power of Saying Yes as a Real Estate Agent...

Saying "yes" as a real estate agent can have a significant positive impact on your business and client relationships. Here are some ways in which the power of saying "yes" can benefit you as a real estate agent:

1. **Building Trust:** When you say "yes" to your clients' needs and requests, you demonstrate your commitment to their satisfaction. This builds trust and rapport, which are essential for long-term client relationships and referrals.

2. **Meeting Client Expectations:** Saying "yes" shows that you are responsive and attentive to your clients' expectations. It can lead to smoother transactions and a better overall experience for your clients.

3. **Problem Solving:** Real estate transactions can involve unexpected challenges. When you say "yes" to addressing these challenges and finding solutions, you show your dedication to overcoming obstacles and ensuring a successful outcome.

4. **Flexibility:** Real estate deals often require flexibility in terms of scheduling, negotiations, and

adjustments. Saying "yes" to accommodating your clients' preferences can make you more adaptable and easier to work with.

5. **Positive Reputation:** Word of mouth is powerful in the real estate industry. When you consistently say "yes" and deliver on your promises, you'll earn a positive reputation, which can lead to more referrals and new clients.

6. **Personalized Service:** Saying "yes" means tailoring your services to each client's unique needs. This personalized approach can set you apart from competitors and create a memorable experience for your clients.

7. **Upselling Opportunities:** Saying "yes" to additional requests or services can lead to upselling opportunities. For example, if a client expresses interest in home staging, you can offer that service to enhance the property's appeal.

8. **Client Loyalty:** Clients appreciate agents who go the extra mile to meet their needs. When you consistently say "yes," you foster client loyalty, making them more likely to work with you again in the future and recommend you to others.

9. **Positive Energy:** A positive attitude and willingness to say "yes" can create a more pleasant and energetic atmosphere during the sometimes-stressful process of buying or selling real estate.

10. **Differentiation:** In a competitive market, your willingness to accommodate your clients' requests and concerns can differentiate you from other agents. This can be a deciding factor for clients choosing an agent to work with.

While saying "yes" can be powerful, it's also important to set boundaries and manage expectations. There may be times when saying "yes" isn't feasible due to legal, ethical, or practical considerations. It's essential to communicate openly with your clients and find the right balance between accommodating their needs and ensuring a successful and compliant transaction.

Being organized is a critical aspect of success in the real estate industry. Real estate transactions involve numerous details, timelines, documents, and client interactions. An organized approach not only helps real estate professionals manage their workload effectively but also enhances client satisfaction, minimizes errors, and boosts overall productivity. Here's an explanation of the power of being organized in real estate:

1. **Efficient Workflow:** Real estate agents juggle multiple clients, properties, appointments, and tasks. An organized workflow ensures that nothing falls through the cracks. Tasks are prioritized, deadlines are met, and clients are provided with prompt responses, enhancing overall efficiency.
2. **Time Management:** Effective organization allows agents to allocate their time wisely. By having a clear schedule, agents can balance prospecting, client meetings, property showings, administrative tasks, and personal time, leading to a better work-life balance.
3. **Client Confidence:** Clients feel more confident working with organized agents. When agents keep

track of details, answer questions promptly, and guide clients through the process seamlessly, it demonstrates professionalism and competence, building trust.

4. **Minimized Mistakes:** Real estate deals involve a plethora of documents, contracts, and legal requirements. Being organized helps agents manage paperwork accurately, reducing the risk of errors that could potentially derail a transaction or lead to legal issues.

5. **Quick Decision-Making:** Organized agents can access relevant information swiftly, enabling them to make informed decisions on behalf of their clients. This agility can be crucial in negotiations and competitive market conditions.

6. **Enhanced Client Experience:** An organized approach translates to a smoother client experience. Clients receive timely updates, have their questions answered promptly, and feel like a priority, leading to higher satisfaction and potential referrals.

7. **Effective Communication:** Being organized ensures that all parties involved in a transaction are on the same page. Whether it's communicating with clients, fellow agents, lenders, or attorneys, organized agents convey information clearly and efficiently.

8. **Adaptability:** The real estate landscape can be unpredictable. An organized agent is better equipped to handle unexpected changes, whether it's adjusting to market fluctuations, addressing

client concerns, or navigating last-minute adjustments.

9. **Networking and Marketing:** Organized agents can maintain detailed records of their contacts, which is crucial for building and nurturing relationships within the real estate industry. They can also execute marketing strategies systematically, leading to better visibility and more leads.

10. **Long-Term Success:** Consistently practicing good organizational habits sets the foundation for a successful and sustainable real estate career. An organized agent is more likely to maintain a strong reputation, repeat business, and referrals over time.

In essence, being organized is a cornerstone of success in the fast-paced and multifaceted world of real estate. It not only improves efficiency but also positively impacts client relationships, decision-making, and overall job satisfaction. Through effective organization, real estate professionals can navigate challenges with confidence and provide the highest level of service to their clients.

So, you may participate in a podcast?

Yes, creating podcasts can be important and beneficial for licensed real estate agents. Podcasts are a versatile and effective medium that allow real estate agents to showcase their expertise, connect with their audience, and differentiate themselves in the competitive industry. Here's why podcasts can be valuable for licensed real estate agents:

1. **Showcasing Expertise:** Podcasts provide a platform for real estate agents to share their knowledge about the market, buying and selling process, investment strategies, and more. This positions them as experts and thought leaders in their field.

2. **Building Credibility:** Consistently producing informative and insightful content through podcasts can enhance a real estate agent's credibility. It shows that they are committed to educating their audience and providing valuable information.

3. **Establishing a Personal Brand:** Podcasts allow real estate agents to establish a personal brand by sharing their unique insights, experiences, and perspectives. This helps them stand out and connect with their audience on a deeper level.

4. **Engaging with Audience:** Podcasts offer a more intimate and personal way to connect with listeners compared to written content. Agents can engage with their audience, answer questions, and address concerns in a conversational manner.

5. **Networking and Collaboration:** Podcasts provide an opportunity to invite guests from related

industries (mortgage brokers, home inspectors, interior designers, etc.) for interviews or discussions. This can lead to valuable networking and collaboration opportunities.

6. **Expanding Reach:** Podcasts have a global reach, allowing real estate agents to connect with listeners beyond their local market. This can be particularly useful if an agent specializes in certain types of properties or investment strategies.

7. **Time-Effective Communication:** Podcasts enable real estate agents to share information effectively in audio format. This can be consumed while listeners are commuting, exercising, or performing other tasks, making it a time-efficient way to reach busy individuals.

8. **SEO and Online Presence:** Publishing podcasts on platforms like Apple Podcasts, Spotify, and Google Podcasts can contribute to an agent's online presence and visibility. Podcasts can also be transcribed and turned into blog posts, further enhancing SEO efforts.

9. **Lead Generation:** Engaging and informative podcasts can attract potential clients who are seeking real estate advice. Listeners who resonate with the agent's content may be more likely to reach out for assistance.

10. **Diversifying Content:** Podcasts provide a different format from written blogs or social media posts. Diversifying content helps keep the audience engaged and interested.

It's important to note that while podcasts can offer numerous benefits, they also require commitment, consistency, and the ability to produce quality content. Real estate agents considering podcasting should ensure they have the resources, time, and enthusiasm to maintain a regular podcast schedule.

Dear Friends and Future Clients,

It is my pleasure to welcome you to this pamphlet, designed to provide you with valuable insights into the world of real estate. Whether you're a first-time agent, a seasoned investor, or someone looking to get into real estate, I am here to guide you every step of the way.

Real estate is more than just transactions; it's about turning your dreams into reality. As your dedicated real estate advisor, I am committed to helping you achieve your goals with professionalism, integrity, and a deep understanding of the market. With that being said, I wanted to dedicate the next set of pages to notes, networking and social media analytics.

NOTES [Blank page, just for you]

Notes [blank page, just for you]

Notes [blank page, just for you]

Notes [blank page, just for you]

Notes [blank page, just for you]

Notes [blank page, just for you]

Notes [blank page, just for you]

Notes [blank page, just for you]

Notes [blank page, just for you]

Notes [blank page, just for you]

Notes [blank page, just for you]